AF517949

LIGHTNING SHOWS THE WAY

LIGHTNING SHOWS THE WAY

J.S. Mishra

BLOOMSBURY
NEW DELHI • LONDON • OXFORD • NEW YORK • SYDNEY

© *J.S. Mishra, 2018*

First published, 2018

All rights reserved. No part of this publication may be reproduced or transmitted in any form or by any means, electronic or mechanical, including photocopying, recording, or any information storage or retrieval system, without prior permission in writing from the copyright holder.

No responsibility for loss caused to any individual or organization acting on or refraining from action as a result of the material in this publication can be accepted by Bloomsbury India or the author/editor.

BLOOMSBURY PUBLISHING INDIA PVT. LTD.
New Delhi London Oxford New York Sydney

ISBN 978-93-86826-62-6

10 9 8 7 6 5 4 3 2 1

Published by Bloomsbury Publishing India Pvt. Ltd.
DDA Complex LSC, Building No. 4, 2nd Floor
Pocket 6 & 7, Sector C
Vasant Kunj, New Delhi 110070

Printed and bound in India by Thomson Press India Ltd.

The content of this book is the sole expression and opinion of its authors, and not of the publishers. The publishers in no manner is liable for any opinion or views expressed by the author. While best efforts have been made in preparing this book, the publishers makes no representations or warranties of any kind and assumes no liabilities of any kind with respect to the accuracy or completeness of the content and specifically disclaims any implied warranties of merchant ability or fitness of use of a particular purpose.

The publisher believes that the contents of this book do not violate any existing copyright/intellectual property of others in any manner whatsoever. However, in case any source has not been duly attributed, the publisher may be notified in writing for necessary action.

To all those
who inspire and enable me
to make my dreams come true.

Contents

Contents

Foreword

Undeniably powerful, poetry has been a life-long companion for me. It's hard to surpass the lyrical intensity of a poem and its ability to capture not just the extraordinary but the poignancy of the ordinary. It gives me incredible joy to see, once again, not just the burgeoning but the transformation of this art form – not just in small circles but as a movement throughout the country. J.S. Mishra is a reminder as to why poetry will always stay alive.

After the meticulous compilation of couplets from eminent Urdu poets, as well as a wonderful translation of these for *Shayaree-e-Zindagee – Poetry for Life*, it is a pleasure to be able to read the work of the man himself. Shri Mishra's eye for details and his ability to capture them on paper ensures that with these poems he makes tangible and brings home a lot of truths.

Reading these poems is like undertaking a journey through his life with all its accompanying hopes, dreams, struggles, and achievements. Evoking strong emotions, they in the process mirror, like all good poetry, one's own life. These poems are indeed a commendable effort by a talented poet.

It truly takes dedication, passion, and a fine sensibility to pen down such lines. May J.S. Mishra's pen never run dry.

Read them in one go or read them in bits and pieces over the days, but read them you must.

17th August 2017
Mumbai

(Javed Akhtar)

Preface

For ages, poetry has been close to the human heart due to its charm and appeal to human sentiments and its effect on the human psyche. Poetry as an art form affects people in the most profound manner and has the capacity to touch the innermost chords of human sensibility. It gives immense joy and inspiration, and enriches the mind and spirit of the readers in a way that no other art form is capable of doing.

Long recognized as an effective medium for deriving joy, inspiration, self-identification, and enriching one's intellect and spirit, poetry beautifully conveys love and affection with passion and intensity. The use of poetry to share one's feelings, emotions, thoughts, and ideas has evolved with human civilization in almost all parts of the world.

In today's life, full of stress and anxiety, it is my conviction that poetry proves to be a great source of respite, inspiration, and strength. As Pablo Naruda says, poetry is an act of peace.

Enabling us to share our joys and sorrow, poetry provides an escape from the mundane turbulence of life's vicissitudes. It inspires us to not only see light at the end of the tunnel but also to light a lamp to ward off the most dense and deep darkness.

With a growing consumerism and the ever expanding scope of technology and innovations leading to an enhanced pace of life, poetry becomes even more important. However, at a time when it as an art form could immensely enrich our lives, I feel that it is increasingly being relegated to the background. It has been observed that children during their formative years are very fond of poems and prefer to read and recite good rhymes and poetry. Unfortunately, as a child grows, exposure to poetry declines and eventually, the stage comes when one is left with hardly any intent or time to read poetry.

Since my school days, I have been interested in Hindi, English, and Urdu poetry. During my student life, both at school and university level, I excessively used Hindi, Urdu, and English poems to buttress and validate my points and arguments during debates and competitions. It helped me in effectively conveying my views and winning many awards and prizes.It has been my interest and endeavour to promote this beautiful art form to the greatest extent possible at my level. Despite the pressure of complex assignments during my three decade long career in the Indian Administrative Service, I have tried to contribute my bit to this great medium of expression. So far, this interest had led to the publication of my six collections of Hindi poems and a collection of Urdu couplets translated into English by me.

'*Lightning Shows the Way*' is my first collection of English poems. Consisting of 52 poems, this collection has poems of various hues and colours. Some of the poems relate to the life and emotions of my twenties, some reflect the intense love and affection shared with my closest family members while others convey the ecstasy of love, deep affection, dreams, ambitions, anxieties, and concerns of daily life.

I am most fascinated with the varied aspects of nature: the sun, the moon, the spectacles of sunrise and sunset, floating clouds, flashes of lightning, beauty of flowers, dignity and calmness of trees, flowing of water, surging of waves, moonlit nights, and ever changing moods of seasons. Some of the poems are reflections of my feelings, emotions, and sense of wonderment regarding these aspects of nature.

Then, there are poems which are the result of spiritual ponderings and a deep sense of enquiry about life and its ways, and the nature and future of human relationships. There are also poems which express my urge to see the world as a place of joy and happiness, where sharing, caring, love, and affection dominate the human psyche and make the world a much better place.

It is my sincere belief that '*Lightning Shows the Way*' would be able to serve the purpose of providing joy and inspiration to readers of varying tastes and interests, as well as remind them of their own memorable moments of life.

10th August 2017 **Jai Shankar Mishra**
Lucknow

Acknowledgements

'*Lightning Shows the Way*', my collection of 52 poems in English, has only been possible due to the sustained support and encouragement of my wife, other family members, and friends.

Completing this journey of penning down my feelings and thoughts, there are a few people who I wish to personally thank for their presence and support.

I wish to express my gratitude to my wife Sharda for providing space, showing patience, sharing deep insights and being the greatest source of strength for more than four decades of our life together.

I wish to express my heartfelt thanks to dear Abhishek, my eldest son, for being an active partner in this creative endeavour, by going through the manuscript and giving valuable suggestions regarding text, title, and cover design.

My sincere thanks goes to my daughter Prashasti, who herself writes beautiful poems, and younger son Divya, who is also a great admirer of poetry, for their appreciation and support by promptly giving their views and suggestions regarding various aspects of the book. I am deeply thankful for their support and encouragement.

My special thanks are due to Alpha Jayanti Singh for her great efforts in editing the manuscript, going through the draft many times over and offering her valuable advice and assistance regarding the text, content, as well as the structure of the poems.

My thanks are also due to Bloomsbury for the great cooperation and understanding shown during the process of finalizing the manuscript and for their excellent efforts in bringing out the book in such an attractive and impressive form.

1

Be New

May new be this sky, this world,
The sun, the moon, and the winds too.
May the rays of the sun have new shine,
The stars, the moonlight – may all be new.

May we have new zeal, new passion,
May there be new rhythm, a new verse.
New be the dawn, new be the nights,
May friends be new, new issues to converse.

May new thoughts, new emotions rule the world,
New facts, new faith, new ways to be told,
May dreams be new, and desires be new,
May prayers be new, may new paths unfold.

May the Himalayas be new, and the Ganga be new,
The notes of affection, the melodies of love be new.
May the Creation be new, and vision be new,
The voices be new, and the songs be new.

•••

2

Dreams

With my dreams, I feel close,
With my dreams, I am intimate,
Dreams speak, although silently,
My dreams, my life's pursuit.

I love dreams, even day-dreaming,
Dreams are my friends, my companions.
Dreams are my complete world,
Dreams are my only possessions.

Whenever I see a lovely dream,
I want to make it my own.
I walk on the dream's path,
Singing a melodious tune.

The dreams that enchanted,
I turned them to reality.
Countless dreams as on-date,
Are, indeed, parts of me.

Fully embracing the dreams,
Being completely immersed in them,
Anointing the dream with fervour,
Worshipping and treating them sacred.

I gained skill in this fine art,
Often, the world has seen it too.
So many dreams, so far in life,
Have been sung and lived through.

•••

3

The Eternal Treasure

Why are my thoughts filled with you,
Every moment, why do you tempt me so.
Ingrained in my soul, in myself,
Eternal but buried deep within,
Why awaken this feeling now and then!

Utterly difficult days and hours,
Sleepless nights, held-up tears,
Singing together on moonlit nights,
All appear in varied layers.
Why do you mean so much to me,
Why is it that you so much love me!

The ways of the world,
The customs of the age,
People's thoughts,
What all they speculate,
Are you really not aware,
Or really not bothered,
And you do not care!

Thoughts forever, meeting never,

And knowing well, we chose!
This urge, longing, deep love,
All that keeps us so close;
To love and never to endorse,
We chose with pleasure,
The most genuine, eternal treasure!

•••

4

My Friend, My Pain

My friend, my pain,
Has come back again.
An old acquaintance,
That was the pretense.

I was ever assured,
With its existence.
May be today or tomorrow,
Sure to happen, visit of the sorrow.

The shades of pleasure,
The shadows of desire,
They kept on weaving,
The web of joy and suffering.

I stumbled, again I stood,
Rose and forward I moved.
Through tranquillity and tempest,
I kept on walking ahead.

Foreseeing the coming of pain,
I always kept on moving.
Knowing the time was approaching,
When again we would be meeting.

The love you have for me,
Is something of which I'm quite aware.
But, I wish to let you know,
Oh Pain, I love you too!

•••

5

Celebrate 'Us'

Which words to choose,
How to convey it to you,
How to let you know,
How to make it explicit,
All that I am in my life,
You are the reason for it.

You pervade my being,
Each and every breath.
You are, indeed, my life.
Despite all the stress and strife,
You bring joy to my heart,
Immense zest, and pure delight.

Hard terrain, countless bends,
Arduous paths, tough and long,
Hand in hand, we walked along!
No respite, absolutely no rest,
See, how far we have come,
Holding on to faith and trust!

How difficult was the journey,
Our paths strewn with thorns,

Challenges, envy, and scorns,
Facing with a smile all the pains,
Through deep and rough oceans,
Sailing together, we could sustain.

This day reminds of our first day,
As true partners in life's journey.
Indeed, it was a new, special day,
A new start, a new life, a new way.
I wish you love and joy on this day,
You have made my life, I wish to say.

May this day of sacred bonds,
Be ever auspicious, ever blessed.
May our further journey be full of light,
May those around, scale great heights,
May nights be cool, our days bright.
May ever, we celebrate and feel delight.

•••

6

Wings and Blessings

How wonderful, that summer-morn!
The earth was mine, the sky was mine,
Entire world was mine, so it seemed,
The fulfilment of all I had ever dreamed.

In my arms was the entire world,
My destiny looked truly in my hold,
The rainbow of my future,
In the horizon seemed so close.

Next to each other, we stood,
Under the shade of the *jamun* tree.
Seeking blessings with stars in our eyes,
Bowing at the mother's feet.

In our journey through life so far,
We have faced times tranquil and tough.
Walking through the mounts and valleys,
We have crossed deserts, vast and rough!

Co-farers, who joined our destiny,
As part of us in life's stream,
Wish to give them, wings and blessings,
And impart them beautiful dreams!

May they be masters of their fate,
May they be captains of their soul.
May these dreams become their treasure,
May their deeds give us pleasure!

•••

7

The Unsung Song

All songs born deep within,
Could not be sung as odes by me,
Endless emotions filled my soul,
Yet I missed the words and tone!

Footsteps of odes were heard coming,
Anguish of creation kept agitating,
Yet the words kept escaping like clouds floating,
Alas, their message could not reach me!

The odes were there in the rays of the sun,
In the fragrance of the flowering season,
In the blowing wind, the glory glowed,
Yet, could not sing your melody in ode!

When flowers bloomed, the moon appeared,
With thunder and lightning, the clouds rained,
I felt your mighty presence, all around,
Yet, you could never be seen or found!

•••

8

Pride and Strength

Such dark hair, like a deep dark night,
Such pretty face, like the moon so bright,
Such simple, affectionate, divine presence,
Such a loving heart, like a blooming lotus.

So much longing, so much affection,
Such deep love, such a great attraction,
How to describe, how to explain,
What all to convey, what all to retain.

The simple innocent words,
Full of zest, joy and substance,
All the feelings, emotions intense,
In your heart and in mine are safe.

This joy that we share together,
This fondness, this love with honour,
The mutual admiration and natural trust,
These are my pride, my strength, my love!

Dedicated to you is everything,
What is there that belongs to me!
Through all eternity and beyond,
May we be together, and retain this bond.

•••

9

Why is it that I Love You So!

What should I call you,
When should I adorn you,
How do I let you know,
Why is it that I love you so.

The dark clouds and winds,
Whenever softly awaken me,
The pitter-patter of the rains,
Remind of you and captivate me.

I go on calling you,
I go on thinking of you.
Oh, why am I so attached,
To memories and thoughts of you.

When the sky is overcast,
With clouds, dark and deep,
When mind starts wandering,
And the body starts dancing,
My heart is never with me,
Why does it go to you,
Oh, how do I let you know,
Why is it that I love you so.

This sweet and pleasant evening,
With promises varied and plenty,
And numerous thoughts and feelings,
Makes the mind wander, never steady.

Why do I imagine your presence,
Why do I suffer your absence so,
Wish you someday realize and know,
Why is it that I love you so.

•••

10

Like a Temple's Idol

With mighty great zeal for life,
Lofty, affectionate mind,
Such loving glances, and so simple,
Cast in sandalwood, like an angel.

You define love, define affection,
Beauty and elegance, in person.
Like a lamp, the glow burns bright,
As if the temple's idol rose to life.

Possessed with a heart of devotion,
Ever restless like Radha and Meera,
Echoing melodies of love and recollections,
Heart and soul immersed in affection.

The words you use, the way you converse,
Are as pure and sacred as a Sanskrit verse,
How to describe your grace and profile,
Your only adornment, a lovely smile.

•••

11

The Song of Love

To you I have dedicated
My love
My affection
My prayers
My complete existence.

Now,
Each song is yours
Each melody is yours
Yours is every word I speak
Yours is every breath I take.

Remember though,
The love I have for you
The love that is only for you
Is everything I have, everything I am.

This love is for you to adorn
This love is for you to cherish
This love is for you to keep safe
This love is for you to caress
Entrusted to you, this love is my treasure.

Some evening,
When the air is fragrant,
with the flowers of night,
When on your roof,
the moon shines bright,
When no-one is around,
And sadness abounds,
Think of me!

Beholding you, calling you,
With all the love, I have for you,
Immersed in the fragrance of flowers,
Bathed in the moonlight showers,
With the same longings,
Of eras and eons,
The same undemanding, unceasing,
Quest for love!

Of many lives, many births,
Tied with the eternal bonds,
I will keep smiling,
I will keep humming,
The song of eternal love,
I will keep singing.

•••

12

The Melancholy

Dejected heart, the same melancholy,
Since evening feeling a deep pain.
The inner voice, the heartbeats say,
You remembered me today again.

I treasure your love with longing,
Recall those moments with deep craving.
My days are full of ecstatic feelings,
And nights, with your thoughts & dreaming.

Intense ache and sadness in the heart,
Mind agitated and burning all over.
The stars, the moon, the blue sky,
Witness to the agony I suffer.

Your love fills every pore of my being,
My poems celebrate your affection.
My heart resounds with your melody,
My eyes well-up on your recollection.

•••

13

Immortal Desire

The affection, the longing, the deep emotions,
They are like a Himalayan stream,
Flowing in the stillness of the night,
As if whispering in the ears of environs:
Love is poetry, a song, music of divinity,
A great blessing, a friend in deep agony.

Love is magic, the fragrance of life,
Though its path is strewn with thorns,
It's a harp whose chords when tinkled,
Write a poem on the canvas of time,
That elevates and rejuvenates forever,
Immortal, indeed, is the desire for love.

It's Sita's patience and Radha's ecstasy,
Gauri's penance and Meera's suffering,
A drop of solidified pain,
With the shell of affection on merging,
Becomes a pearl of eternal of devotion.
Immortal, indeed, is the desire for love.

•••

14

The Beauty of You

Magic like touchstone, pure as sandal,
Your presence always emanates fragrance.
In the chaos of this everyday life,
You are a symbol of support and patience.

The innate calmness and great serenity,
Cool intellect, composure and gravity.
Your thoughts, grace, spell and charm,
All great harbours in life's storm.

Every moment, I feel your presence,
All the time I feel lonely without you.
On every cue, I hear your footsteps,
My heart warms up just thinking of you.

My life rejuvenates because of you,
You fill my heart, you fill my soul.
The passion and charm is so heightened,
With you around, every corner is lightened.

You are cool as, indeed, is the moon,
Your splendour like the rays of the sun.
Incarnation you are of candour and purity,
Of beauty you are the true definition.

All my songs, all music of mine,
Because of you are admired and loved.
The divinity and blessings, all the beauty,
Everything in life is because of you.

•••

15

A New Dawn

Life complicated, forsaken and deserted,
Flourished again, as the seasons changed.
Found the moon, the sun, and the stars,
Life's wavering boat moved to a safe shore.

The stars sparkled bright in the sky,
Times changed, new life gained.
With you by my side, with us being together,
Found the treasure I thought was lost forever.

My life! What a storm, what a tempest,
Hardly a life, only breathing at best.
Still with a smile on the lips always,
Kept bearing the pain, night and day.

A new smile now plays on my lips,
Unaware of how the time flies by.
Now life is full of love and charms,
I have the whole world in my arms.

The dark days over, now laughter and fun,
Basking in the glory of a bright new sun.
New buds opened, new flowers bloomed,
To new melodies, my life is now tuned.

The joy and zeal have reached new heights,
My life now is full of love's fragrance.
The dreams and passions of eras bygone,
Are in my embrace indicating a new dawn.

•••

16

I Find You All Around

Why does the heart pine for you,
Why in life so much delusion,
Is this the climax of passion,
Or merely longing's reflection.

Why have you come in my life,
Why so much agony and strife,
You seem to have forgotten me,
Yet, agitated is my whole being!

Is this love, affection or longing,
Passion, liking, the heart's yearning.
Is this the ache and worry of losing,
Or is it the omen of our meeting!

An infatuation of the eyes and lips,
Of the stolen glances, lovely eyelids,
Of smiles, so hesitant and shy,
Of curls, dark as clouds in the sky.

Is it the obsession of sweet voice,
Of the passionate feelings of many births,
Unsatiated, restless and frozen,
Of innate longing, the symbol eternal.

Is it the passion you emanate
Or the enchanting ways of your speaking
Immersed in the sweetness so bewitching
Although often reluctant and hesitating.

This thought now fills my mind
Where did it begin, how it ended,
Whether the magic of beauty and grace
Could really so charm a traveler of distance.

This charm, lure and enchantment,
In the midst of all turmoil in life,
Not physical it is, but a soul connection,
Of deep love, support and affection.

A part of my being, I treasure you,
I find you all around me.
You are in my thoughts and in my dreams,
The reason of my life, my poems' themes.

•••

17

Tell Me All

Tears in the eyes,
Pain in the heart,
Why so much distress,
Why this severe pain!
Tell me all about it.

Why this weariness,
The burning sensation,
Why eyes are filled with tears,
Why this hurt, all these fears!
Tell me all about it.

Where have gone,
The zeal and joys,
The spring in gait,
The songs and melodies!
Tell me all about it.

What burns your heart,
Why so much agitation,
With tears rolling down,
Why this isolation!
Tell me all about it.

You permeate the earth and sky,
A true soul-mate, my sole ally,
You fill my heart, you fill my soul,
Why don't you realize your place and role!
Tell me all about it.

•••

18

Tides of Emotions

Shriveled and shrunk,
The dark gray clouds,
The expanding vast sea,
Likewise in my heart,
Thoughts and feelings,
Numerous dreams,
Varied conversations,
Transient relations,
All agitating like deviant waves!
Wide sky, expansive and high,
The restless sea, energetic and wild,
Fickle, playful, naughty waves,
All resonating in the heart, time and again.

The blue, serene leaning sky,
Horizon coming near and closer,
Endless waves rushing to the shore,
The sea so enormous, mysterious,
Unknown movements, immense depths,
So captivating, the youthfulness of waves.

Moving forward, surging ahead,
Same paths, same destinations,

Rising and falling again and again,
Reaching the shore and turning away,
Sulking and upset, backing away,
Erasing their identity, their existence,
Sprawling and scattering time and again.

Heart's zeal and waves of the sea,
Alike in nature, thoughts and actions,
The tides of emotions and longings,
Over and over again they rise,
Incessantly, thousands of times.
The heart's sky, and varied thoughts,
The emotions, aspirations, all its parts,
Like waves they are, in actions, in nature,
Totally similar in form and feature.

•••

19

The Symbol of Love

This symbol of love,
Through its marbles,
What is it that it speaks?

Stones don't have a voice,
Reunion never happens,
God only is worthy of devotion,
Merging with Him, the aim of life.

Yet,
The stones of Taj Mahal speak!
Why do they speak,
What do they speak,
Do they cry or sing?
What's their caste, religion,
race and language,
What message do they really convey?

So much love for his wife,
Such a great attraction,
Many years of grieving, crying,
Immense pain, unbearable wailing,
All in an Emperor's heart,

Through years and eternity.
Dream for a grand memorial,
Strong will to realize the dream.
This curiosity, this eagerness to know,
Everyone with the question same,
Be it an artist, an author, a householder,
Or an adolescent, young and old, all of them.

On the canvas of time,
This memorial, is a pearl of love,
Or engraved on every grain of stones,
All over, it's a song of love!
Without words, without a language,
How do these stones speak?
How do they communicate?
This is indeed, an unsolved mystery.

I saw on the bank of Yamuna,
Speaking, singing, humming stones,
The constant pursuit of a dream,
An embodiment of what the mind conceived.
Built on a promise there stands,
A relic of deep love, and true affection!
A living monument of life's longings,
Of deep sentiments and pure emotions.
I saw it all in the palace of love,
I saw the Taj Mahal!

I saw here,
The breeze of love and sweet memories,
Varied hues and colours of passion,

The blazing ways of living life,
In every nook and corner,
Pervading the air and environs, everywhere.
From the entry of the premises and its avenues,
To the walls and steps, and in latticed windows,
I saw the love drifting, floating,
Peeping and whispering,
At times smiling, laughing,
Sometimes weeping, sometimes singing.

The monument speaks loud and clear,
In this short span of life,
Granted to us on the planet earth,
Is all the conflict, envy and discord,
Really worth it, has it any sense?
Why do we not celebrate,
Mutual liking, affection and love,
Why do we not care and caress,
And beautify the bonds of love!

•••

20

You are the Breeze

You are right here, so close to me,
You are the air, you are the breeze.
At the door, in the room, in the courtyard,
In every splendour, in the beauty of flowers.
In each breath, in each beat of the heart,
Pervading the core of my being,
All over, everywhere you are.

I saw you coming, pausing - slightly hesitating,
I saw you smiling, singing, and humming,
You are right here, so close to me,
You are the air, you are the breeze.

You are around, in moments of elation,
In affection, in love, in the colours of passion,
In melodies, in songs, in the music all around,
In each step, each moment, pervading my soul.
You are right here, so close to me,
You are the air, you are the breeze.

•••

21

Lightning Shows the Way

In adverse moments of life,
Your are with me, are close to me,
The days of despair, depressing nights,
The anguish and distress,
Long and tedious moments, emptiness all around,
In all directions deep darkness abounds,
A world of despair vast and endless,
A world of agony and painfulness.

When the storms come to life
When clouds thunder, lightning strikes,
When the path is strewn with thorns,
And nothing can be seen anywhere,
Then all of a sudden,
Coming from somewhere, someone quietly,
Holds my hands, holds me close,
And rekindles the desire to live.
Like in dark deep nights,
To a wayfarer lost and lonely,
The way is shown by the lightning bright.

•••

22

Together We have Been

Holding on to hopes with patience,
Entangled in the web of time,
Seconds appeared long as days,
The days to months stretched.
And then, my dear friend,
This day has finally arrived.

Valleys and valleys, as far as we can see,
In the eyes, only dreams and dreams abound.
Such an exquisite moment, ambience like heaven,
The earth, the horizon, blue and serene all around.

Passing through storms, we reached so far,
Everything a result of our thoughts and deeds.
It seems this bond is not of this life alone,
Through many births, together we have been!

•••

23

Never Shed Tears

Of the same colour,
Are affection and love,
Agony and pain too,
Bear the same colour.
Complementing each other,
For centuries together,
Visible, invisible,
Their bond eternal.

Only one wish, only one prayer,
Those, strung with love's thread,
May they be ever happy and blessed,
May their eyes never have tears to shed.

May you have patience and composure,
May there be glory, strength and vigour,
Take this pledge, give me your words,
Despite great pain, you will never shed tears.

•••

24

Only One Vision

Holding on to strings of dreams,
Being together, high in the sky,
O what a wonderful wish is this,
A lovely desire to fly.

Everything blue,
For as far as we could see,
With flying and floating clouds,
Will float hearts, yours and mine.

So many dreams woven,
Together, since ages,
So many flowers picked,
From the garden of love and affection.

The heart of this world,
Alas, is not so large,
As to understand this bond,
And appreciate the love in our hearts.

Letting go the deceits of the times,
A new dawn should now arise,
With gifts of love and good will,
Surround us all, and surprise.

Now, only one vision,
A new earth, we all envision,
Where everybody is happy and free,
And there is suffering for none.

•••

25

Eras will Sing

The one with a heart full of zeal,
The one with innumerable dreams,
The one who endeavours day and night,
To make everyone enjoy glory and bliss.

Who brings cheers, just being close,
Comfort even whose memories evoke,
Who has fully devoted to the world,
Each moment, his heart and soul.

With whom young and old easily relate,
Who delights his friends and colleagues,
Who is willing to help the sad and sombre,
And is dear to all, young and elder.

Whose footsteps are engraved in stones,
Whose legend is writ large on waves,
This earth is his, and the sky is his,
He is the leader, real hero in essence.

He with his thoughts and actions,
Will transform the earth into heaven,

And will reign over the hearts of the nation,
Beyond the boundaries of states and regions.

He is the one whose legend eras will sing,
And on whom the world will shower its blessings.

•••

26

Wake Up

O traveler,
Why do you not remember your aim,
How entangled in passions, in dreams!
The night has set so long ago,
All the stars have disappeared too.
Yet, you are still asleep in your bed,
The moon kept close, beside your head.

Wake up, move on, the night has gone,
Arising from the horizon, is a new dawn,
Wake up, wake up and hear,
The echoes of time, in your ears,
Why lost are you still,
In the sweeps of your dreams.

•••

27

Life is a River

To move ahead or stop,
To set out or wait,
To do or not,
What all to be sought?

The threads of life,
Entangled in various ways,
In different bonds, relations,
In varied feelings, emotions!

The passage of life,
Is not a straight line,
But a circle too,
It's not, is true!

With its fun and frolic,
Its rises and falls,
Through lives and deaths,
Skipping through eons and ages.

It has been flowing,
Over plain and rugged terrain,
Life is a river on its journey,
Moving towards eternity.

•••

28

Seize the Day

Taking a vow to walk ahead,
On a new path, in mid journey,
Make efforts and be awakened,
Commit yourself, night and day.

Only hard work leads to success,
Nothing is attained without efforts,
Life becomes sublime by exertions,
With hard work, the closed door opens.

Efforts lead to bridges on seas,
Efforts make a new world possible,
Ascent of Everest, churning of ocean,
With sincere efforts, all became achievable.

Having divinity, and power within,
Awake and arise, fulfill your dreams,
Use each moment and march ahead,
Seize the night, seize the day!

•••

29

The Lonely Life

What kind of agony, day and night,
Why do storms, surge and swell.
Why so lonely, is the life,
What goes on, in sub-conscious mind?

When in life, the waves of love,
Drench the body, drench the soul.
When emotions of love resonate,
And create, a life, so wonderful!

When love embraces the life,
When songs flow, from the lips.
When nature adorned as a bride,
Fascinates both, the body and mind.

When fragrance of *Rajnigandha,*
Overwhelms, each pore of the being.
When flowers get sprinkled on the ground,
With Harsingar's branches quivering.

When love, deep and intense,
Overpowers, the body and heart,
Why so much pain arises in the soul,
When cuckoo coos in the nights so dark!

Life, indeed, is a lonely journey,
Yet, the eternal dilemma persists,
Why so lonely, is the life,
What goes on, in sub-conscious mind?

•••

30

May Love Reign Supreme

Anxiety with each moment, each step,
Unending race, day and night,
Yet life is sweet, in its up and down ways,
The moon and the stars, let us embrace.

The twists and turns of time,
All entangled, in life's journey,
How pleasant is the vault of blue sky,
There is a world beyond the human eye!

I wish to live in calm environs,
Where days and nights stand still,
Where breezes sing, peace prevails,
Where stars whisper, and love reigns.

When buds snap, and bloom into flowers,
Sweet melody floats, and heart wanders.
When clouds gather, and glide in the sky,
Nature celebrates, woods dance and sway.

When peacocks spread their wings, may there be rains,
Swayed on the rhythm of dance, may time cease to exist.
May days be celebratory, nights festive,
May love reign supreme, be the greatest gift.

•••

31

Give Wings to Love

The lovely colours of the rainbow,
The dark and dense floating clouds,
The fragrant breeze, all signs of love,
Signifying love's devotion, deep affection.
Love is a song from deep within,
Love is a feeling, love is a blessing.
Give wings to love, never hinder it,
Never bind love down, follow it.

Love is the purpose of life,
Love is the message of life,
Love is the reason of existence,
Love is the fragrance of life's essence.
Love is an echo, a quiet conversation,
Love is a resonance of two emotions.
Give wings to love, never hinder it,
Never bind love down, follow it.

All attachments left aside,
All likes and dislikes of life,
Let love reign supreme, be our guide,
In the morn and eve, let love pervade,

The days and nights, let love embrace.
Give wings to love, never hinder it,
Never bind love down, follow it.

May all worship only love,
May all dance to the tune of love,
May love's fragrance fill the air,
May love's echo reverberate forever.
Love is, indeed, a great freedom,
Love is a new birth, a divine wisdom.
Give wings to love, never hinder it,
Never bind love down, follow it.

•••

32

Fly High in the Sky

So much anxiety in heart and soul,
So many questions arising in mind,
Since the decision to leave and go,
Heartbeats increased, tears rolled.

The decision followed deep thoughts,
Consensus emerged to move ahead,
Now, when the moment arrived,
So much agitation in the mind!

The earth, the sky, all the world,
Prompted to move ahead, on a new path,
Sea waves seemed to call me close,
Urging to find a new vision, a new source.

To stay in comfort, is no destiny,
Life is an eternal quest, each day and night,
To kiss the mounts, the summits are calling,
And so is the call of the waves in the sea.

Open thy arms, fly high in the sky,
With countless dreams in your heart,
Touch new heights, new horizons,
With new friends, to new destinations.

•••

33

Transcending All Limits

Whenever I am alone, with myself,
I find you close, always by my side.
With a sweet smile on your lips,
You embrace my presence, my whole being.

From the bonds of this world,
When I get free, now and then,
World around fascinates immensely,
Nature captivates, so fresh and lovely.

Thoughts in many hues and colours,
Engulf my conscious with your presence,
In tune with my songs, breeze also sings,
World gets engulfed in this magic breathtaking.

Thunder of clouds, incessant rains,
Lonely moments, deep dark nights,
Cause, a strange mix of love and pain,
I get lost, in delightful memory-lane.

Despite stress and distress of life,
Flowers seem spread along the passage,
The ecstasy of our youthful days,
Overwhelms the mind and spreads.

The heart seems possessed with love,
As if walking above the ground,
Or floating above, high in the sky,
Transcending all limits, I wish to fly.

During these moments, all of a sudden,
I find you near, extremely close,
With a sweet smile on your lips,
You embrace my presence, my whole being.

•••

34

Moving with the Moon

Last night, I kept moving with the moon,
All night, moonlight enveloped creation,
But pain accumulated in the heart,
Kept on agitating for its expression.

When I saw the moon in the evening,
In my mind arose thousands of images,
Of love, passion, grief and suffering,
Pages from my memory-book, kept on opening.

In my heart surged tides of agony,
Pain flowed in the form of poetry,
Echoing the love and grief of ours,
And the longing to touch the stars.

During the night, moving with the moon,
One thing led to another, and kept stirring,
The pain and ecstasy, of the eras gone,
Melted into poems and kept on flowing.

•••

35

New Poems on New Pages

Like the leaves of autumn, one day,
Sure it is that I will go away.
Having played my role on the world's stage,
With me, my dreams will also drift away!

When phase of life takes new turns,
And memories seem hazy and fading,
When new dreams surge in your being,
New visions prompt, and look tempting.

Write new poems, on new pages,
Which inspire people, old and young,
And appeal to millions and resonate,
And reverberate through times and ages.

Such new poems, I couldn't create,
This pain is there, this agony persists,
The heart says, to you I entrust the dream,
Yet, the wisdom forbids, and stops me!

Fully aware I am, the ways of destiny,
Can never be easily altered and swayed,
But the dreams passed on, day and night,
Are indelible, and can never be erased.

•••

36

We will Sing Together

When rainbow appears in the sky,
When wonderful images charm,
When fragrance spreads all over,
When new songs flow, and overpower.

When blueness of the sky, so vast,
Overwhelms the body and the heart,
When dark clouds gather and the rain pours,
When my being gets drenched to the core.

Whenever the beauty of the cosmos,
Touches my heart, quite deep within,
And playful surging waves of the sea,
Soak my heart and body completely.

When sweet melody of a song,
Ensues from my lips, and resonates,
When in garden, fragrance permeates,
And beauty blooms and fills the space.

I wish, in such moments of life,
You were close, together with me,
This could be possible, that could be done,
In ecstatic moments, anything could happen!

These moments, these emotions,
Feelings of the heart, its impressions,
Etched in conscious, the joy and strife,
Sustain each moment, the journey of life!

I have only one dream, one desire,
If the destiny brings us close, ever,
We will live these moments,
We will sing these songs together!

•••

37

The Poem

How should I write such a poem,
Which enthuses the body and soul,
Which truly echoes the severe pain,
And suffering; fulfilling its basic role.

That which reflects the barbs and jeer,
Human anguish and agony in every letter,
Whose each line is filled with tears,
Yet that helps people fight slight and fear.

Despite fiercely dark clouds in the sky,
Indicating storm and tempest in life,
Despite the thunder and lightning,
The poem that uplifts the heart and mind.

Despite the high and mighty waves,
Coming to the shore, with frightful roar,
Even for one, having support of none,
The poem that makes the life worthwhile.

A poem that fills the heart with joy,
That invigorates body and soul,
That enlightens life's course,
That elevates it and drives with force.

•••

38

New Zeal, New Passion

Morning and evening, day and night,
Each and every moment together,
I feel semblance of your presence,
Here, there and everywhere.

Every breath, every move in life,
Each step of journey, dark or bright,
Has a sense of your proximity.
Each moment is filled with love and light.

Your presence pervades my dreams,
Even walking alone, I feel you close,
Without speaking a single word,
My heart is filled with thoughts of yours.

Whenever I am tired, tormented,
I find comfort in your divine presence,
Arise, awake and win glory,
Eternal words, spread their fragrance.

I find new energy, a new vision,
New zeal, new vigour, and new passion,
Each and every cell of my body,
My heart and my mind, with lightning sparkle.

•••

39

Joy for Everyone

How much water has flown in rivers,
How much water passed through streams,
How much distance still to go,
How much time, there still remains!

One who lived only for himself,
Life filled with pride and deceit,
Will he appreciate the life's gifts,
Of love true and affection genuine!

In this great journey of life,
What all was exchanged, lost and found,
Why not pause for a moment and ponder,
Was it a life, or did only dreams abound!

A meaningful life is said to be one,
Where joy is there for everyone,
Not only this world but all existence,
Is truly intimate and our very own!

•••

40

My Poems, My Recourse

To face the struggles of life,
The thunder of clouds dark and deep,
Countless questions, doubts aplenty,
My poems - my recourse only.

My poems, the accompanying music,
Each and every word with its sound,
Electrifies and invigorates my life,
Howsoever stormy the days and nights.

In life, hatred and anger all around,
Envy, fear, and delusion verily surround,
Deserted paths, rugged terrain,
My own poems-my only support and strength!

May these poems float in the air,
May they wander free in the environs,
May the sound resound in valleys and peaks,
And spread joy in the world all over.

May essence ofVedas echo in my poems,
May wisdom of Upnishads reflect therein,
May my poems convey Meera's suffering,
May they have Radha's love overflowing!

All sacred thoughts and blessings,
All sincere efforts for earth's well being,
May all these keep on echoing forever,
This is my only dream, my only desire.

•••

41

Life is a Song

Life is a song, life is love,
A stream of time, running and flowing,
It is the glow of the morning-sun,
An expanse of desires-eternal, ever-lasting.

Life is the mighty flow of a surging river,
Yet at times, the receding tide it is,
With countless dreams and promises,
It is a celebration, a gift it is!

Life is a song, poetry and prose,
Adorning the earth, embellishing the world,
Elevated to the sky if it moves ahead,
But if it gets lost, merely a business!

•••

42

Today, All Over Again

Today, all over again,
Your memories engulf me,
Today again the songs we loved,
I started humming.

The promise was there,
Joy and grief-all we'll share,
You will sing my songs,
With grace and flair.

That, whenever my thoughts,
Will fill your mind,
You will hum the tunes,
And sweetly smile.

That, with the brush of love,
On the canvas of life,
All seven colors of the rainbow,
You will fondly apply.

Every new phase in life,
Kept on calling me,
Every melody in the journey,
Kept on enthralling me.

Each day, every night,
Every moment in life always,
I kept on finding you,
And, losing you, again!

Few steps only we walked,
When the season changed,
And, the clouds in the sky,
Gathered and swelled.

The flashes of lightning,
Suddenly set ablaze,
All desires and dreams,
Lost fervour, lost craze.

Ecstasy of those moments,
Today, all over again,
Torments the soul, causing,
Great agony, very deep pain.

The same old tunes and songs,
I like humming again and again,
Despite life's twists and turns,
You make me smile, and sustain.

•••

43

Spread Far and Wide

May your mind be as elevated as peaks,
May your virtues endear elders and colleagues,
May your repute resemble a banyan tree,
May the wealth be your thoughts and deeds.

May your heart have the depth of seas,
May you always spread grace and light,
May you stand forever for truth and right,
May you inspire in others love and delight.

May your fame spread far and wide,
May it reverberate through all the ages,
May you stand for the noble values,
Long established by our ancient sages.

•••

44

Touch the Stars

On the horizon of desire, at twilight,
When the beautiful rainbow faded,
The dream flying high in the sky,
Broke away and the heart saddened.

The eyes were set on the moon and stars,
With intent desire, a deep passion.
Why this pain then for the setting sun,
Or for the rainbow, that sparkles on the horizon.

But a web of rays is this rainbow,
A beautiful play of colours.
Hiding in the deep dark clouds at times,
So is the way of this amazing beauty.

Old is its game of hide and seek,
Momentary is its dazzling view.
Never was it your destination, your aim,
Higher set were the goals by you.

Recall now the longing you had,
Of reaching the stars in the sky.
Reawaken yourself with a renewed zeal,
Forget the despair of the night gone by.

Awake, arise, and march ahead,
Touch the moon and stars so bright.
May your fame be like the rising sun,
The stars in your hands; hold them tight.

•••

45

What is Life?

What is life?
Is life prose, poetry, or fiction,
A narration of life's events, griefs, and joys,
Is it to promote the good and sacred,
An occasion to spread joy and light,
Or is it for earning glory and repute,
An opportunity for worldly pursuit.

What is life?
Is this life a journey of joy,
Is it to strive for ultimate salvation,
Is life meant for joy and celebration,
Or is it a great burden- a forced situation!
Is it just a sequence of days and nights,
Or an opportunity to revere beauty and delight.

What is life?
Is life a love song or a riddle to solve,
Is its objective to earn name and fame,
To work for victory in every game.
Or is it merely a series of acts,
Played out on the stage of life.
Is it the nectar of immortality,
Or a poison to suffer and survive.

•••

46

Rhythm and Vigour

Spirits soared, millions of bells rang,
When the evening began turning young,
All around spread the beauty and brilliance,
Music and songs made their appearance.

The fragrant flowers, so very colourful,
Made the setting grand and beautiful,
Bright and quivering lamps lit for welcome,
Danced and greeted the graceful blossoms.

How wonderful is the flowers' world,
In moments and days, the life captured,
Life devoted to beauty and delight,
With sole aim to spread joy and light.

In the lovely setting of music and colours,
Many took the floor with rhythm and vigour,
Body and soul filled with youthfulness,
Everywhere floated joy and happiness.

•••

47

The Earth and Heaven

The obstructions in the path of life,
Why do they distress so much,
The bondage of action and inaction,
Appears so complex and tangled.

Agitation at every step,
So much misery and suffering around,
Every moment full of anxiety,
Total lack of compassion and piety.

For how long can we be mute spectators,
How can the sufferings come to an end,
Existence is eternally calm and cheerful,
But the human being, ever stressed and fearful.

What to do, how to move ahead,
How to change the scene and settings,
How to make the world a heaven on earth,
How to make life full of joy and worth.

Doubts, fear and poverty surround,
Divisions and mistrust rule the day,
All involved in this losing game,
A heavy price we are bound to pay.

May everyone have a worthy life,
May the world become a place of love,
May everybody be happy and joyful,
When will in all such wishes develop.

May this earth be free from suffering,
May everyone share the riches of life,
May the planet earth turn into heaven,
May we follow the words of saints and sages.

●●●

48

Since Eras and Eons

Having the wings of love,
Let's fly and touch the horizon,
Let's spread the songs of longing,
To every home, forest, and garden.

The songs which change the world,
The songs which charm one and all,
The songs which tell the glory of love,
And bring everyone to its beck and call.

The songs burst forth from the lips,
Hearing the melody of the nightingale,
The songs which inspire love and joy,
And become part of a true love-tale.

Flowing of water and ways of love,
Facing all hurdles, flouting constraints,
Have been the same since eras and eons,
Ever flowing ahead defying restraints.

Why to honor and follow old rules,
Rules that hurt, and limit the flight,
Let us realize the power of love,
And fly high with all our might.

•••

49

With Verve and Fervour

Having you by my side in life,
Life is joy, poetry and rhyme,
New warmth of love each moment,
New dawn, new days and nights.

Even on life's rugged path,
There's light in the darkest hour,
The rainbow emerges from the clouds,
Giving new zeal, energy, and power.

New dreams, new paths, new zest,
Enthuse life to march ahead,
Search new horizons, and islands new,
New vistas, environs, new world widespread.

Be it a tempest or life's humdrum,
Days of glum, joy, or great honour,
Taking into stride all seasons alike,
Let's live life with verve and fervour.

•••

50

Sing with Me

When will you come and be with me,
When will you learn to sing with me.

Each moment in life, just one desire,
Just one dream, one burning fire,
Day and night, conscious-subconscious,
The body and mind ever cautious,
Sitting on the banks of the stream of life,
Will you like this waste your time.

When will you come and be with me,
When will you learn to sing with me.

Each and every word, every breath,
Every song echoes your longing,
All the pain and sufferings in life,
Stressful days and anxious nights,
Reigning doubts, floating queries,
When will you come and sort them out.

When will you learn to sing with me,
When will you come and be with me.

•••

51

I Remember

All your yearnings and sufferings,
To me you think is not known,
But rest assured, all your sorrows,
Are fully shared, never unknown.

The joy and zest of days gone by,
The nights so cool, days so bright,
Sweet memories of the time together,
Equally haunt me day and night.

Walking together in endless rains,
Under deep dark clouds, thunder and light,
Unconcerned with the ways of the world,
Its turns and bends, its rules and might.

It all seems a series of dreams,
Seen in a long deep dark slumber,
That came to a naught on waking-up,
All the grief and pain- I fully remember.

•••

52

The Ceaseless Journey

During all the struggles and the storms,
Without any quiver, the lamps lit bright,
Clouds kept surging and swelling wild,
Yet, I moved ahead, with grit and might.

There was no one around to help and support,
The paths were rugged, with thorns strewn,
Dense, deep forests covered the way,
There was heavy downpour, incessant rain.

Deterring and difficult mountain-peaks,
Beautiful flowers and lovely terrain,
All enticing to pause, to halt and relax,
Yet, with clear vision, I opted to march on.

No shelter, no shade on the way,
No partner, no companion around,
Many obstacles, bends and turns,
Yet new paths, new ways were found.

Despite the pain and suffering in life,
Through all the thunder, rain and storm,
With dreams, and courage to fulfill them,
I marched ahead with determined calm.

This ceaseless journey is now my fate,
Joy and hope for all is the aim,
Moving with time is now not an option,
To push time forward is the only game.

•••